Heart Crafted Poems

MUSINGS OF AN OLD MAN

JLR

Table of Contents

Section 3 ~ *Memories*

Section 4 ~ *Retrospections*

Dedicated to my grandchildren:
Brad, Eric, James, John, Morgan, Evan,
Makala, and Elizabeth.

Special thanks to my dear friend Connie,
who helped ignite the poetic flame for
these words to be found in my heart;
and to Diane, my writing coach, who created
a safe place for me to become one with my
feminine side.

But my guiding light in the development
of these words is my soulmate, Bonnie,
who encouraged me and selflessly gave me
the time to write.

Musing — *deeply or seriously thoughtful; "the persona of a an old man;" Contemplative, meditative, pensive, pondering, reflective, ruminative, brooding, broody, spiritual, loving, yearning.*

"Painting is poetry that is seen rather than felt, and poetry is painting that is felt rather than seen." — LEONARDO DA VINCI

SECTION 1

Contemplations

Passion

To be bound
impetuously
in love's grasp

Falling jewels

Jewels shine brightly,
stars beaming nightly.
Beads tarnish, turn dull.
Stars from sky fall.

Golden rings gleam,
moonstone beam.
Diamonds
Sapphire
Topaz
Pearl
each
one
shines
glows
gleams
flares.
But the stars
that fall …
go dark.

Dreams unfold

Dreams unfold, casting nets at distant stars!
Grasping glittering hopes to fill our souls.
Harvest of hopes sliding alongside Mars,
dreams unfold, casting nets at distant stars!

A sprinkling of stardust healing life's scars,
while into Eden's lush garden, we stroll.
Dreams unfold, casting nets at distant stars.
Grasping glittering hopes to fill our souls.

Rhinoceros

Rhinos are passive giants.
I ask, "how could one not love these?"
Two-inch-thick skin,
not pliant,
four legs like trunks of trees.
Rhino's more massive
than defiant,
impassive.

But don't push!

Winnowing winter winds

Winnowing winter winds,
whoosh, the trees breathe in the air
stirred by clouds rushing across the sky.

Rustling, wilted leaves deftly,
with a dare of the wind,
rush ever brisker, harder try.

Winnowing winter winds, swirling layers of decay.
Leaves defoliating, carried upward on air currents,
floating, twirling down from the tallest branches,
feather-like rocking back and forth in slow-motion.

Seeing the wavering bark flit off the birch's trunk,
seeking drops of water for absorption.

Winnowing winter winds, gentle winds
and winter seize hold of time.

Calm winds and winter's grip relax.
A steady breeze is rattling the largest of chimes.

Willowing breeze, winter season waxes.

Raindrops crescendo

I awoke to gray skies this morn,
lingering stiffness is my bane.
Aged, frail, my emotions forlorn.
Raindrops crescendo off the pane.

Winters seem to linger longer.
With gentle rains tapping refrain
wanting sunlight brighter, stronger.
Raindrops crescendo off the pane.

The little wren with feathers soaked
sits with rain, cleansing his domain,
flitting his wings to shake the wet away.
Raindrops, crescendo off the pane.

The morning hours pass, still I plea
to let the sun's rays, dance again.
Asking the wren to please, agree!
Raindrops crescendo off the pane.

Not so ordinary Gold

All that glitters is not Gold, but
the Gold that glitters is desired more.

Gold, it has been said, "is the King's ransom."
But is it so?

Gold, more handsome and pure,
is melted in the fiery cauldrons
to become glorified coins, treasured.

Consider, however, Gold spun by the honey bee.
Perhaps containing more wealth,
per gram, than pure Gold,
when counting the number of bees
collecting the nectar from God's flora.

Or, one might include the Gold in the
medals of athletes who compete and
then measure the sweat and training.
The real value of their coveted treasure.

Or, when bands of Gold are heaven kissed
to bind the tie of two souls entwined.
These precious symbols have no price.

Or, the Gold dust that comes with stardust dreams,
as the alchemist hopes to mix
vials so full, so perchance his schemes will succeed.

Last but not least, the golden stairs,
that we expect to ascend in peace-filled glory
when we come to the end of our journey.

Angels' tears

Just imagine with me …

for eons upon eons,
an innumerable multitude of
angels shed a single tear
for those brave heavenly souls,
who decided to give being human a try!

Time passed, the oceans grew with each new tear.

With a resounding plink … another angel
dropped to earth through birth,
adding one more human being, so dear.
As hosts of angels in the heavens above,

witnessed the human experience unfold,
replete with highs and lows,
sadness and laughter aches to turn to pains,
joys, sorrows, and yes, losses.

Angels above cheered on these earth-bound celestials,
living Life as humans doing human things.
Marveling at the sheer determination of those below,
as their days on earth continued to flow.

All the while, this human experience was
in continuous transition,
while these journeyers learned Life's lessons
of doing, being, seeing what human Life entails.
Noting most of all, that earthly Life is so opposite
of Heaven's conditions.

In the Garden of Rest, a peaceful space,
they knew Love not hate, acceptance not rejection,
calmness not stress, discernment not ignorance,
tolerance not bigotry, unanimity not disagreement.

What a wonderment it is then
when a human have had enough of this
earth-bound experiment!

They leave their earthly human vessel,
and resounding cheers and claps
are heard across the heaven scape …
as multitudes of Angelic hosts
welcome these sojourners home, unscathed.

Spinning, twisting, turning

Around this spinning, twisting, turning globe
you thought you were the only one who,
each day saw the moon, the sun.

Above this spinning, twisting, turning globe
you thought you were the only one
who, every day, had battles to be won.

Beneath this spinning, twisting, turning globe
you thought you were the only one
who had concerns of our damage done.

Beside this spinning, twisting, turning globe
You thought you were the only one
to see our moral principles undone.

Inside this spinning, twisting, turning globe
we swirl, we twirl, we wobble, we hobble
from birth to death, we run and run and run!

Wading in thought

Wading upstream
water rushing,
sparkling moonbeams.
Thoughts come gushing,
ruddy face flushing,
my pulse streams.

I wake from the dream!

If only

Dr. King:

If only people could open the doors
to where your departed soul rests!

Replay your voice, hear again your powerful,
passionate plea for man to see
more clearly man's inhumanity to man.

If only people could open the doors
to where your departed soul rests!

Simply because we need
to hear again
and yet again …
"judge not the color of a person's skin."

If only people could open the doors
to where your departed soul rests!

To hear the cries that you and yours heard.
The pleas …
"please see me,
see who I am,
do not see the color of my skin."

If only people could open the doors
to where your departed soul rests!

To see the tear-streaked faces
of mothers losing sons,
of mothers losing daughters
of wives losing husbands,
because of the color of their skin.

If only people could open the doors
to where your departed soul rests!

To taste the vile words spoken
with such hate, such anger!
Entirely out of complexities
about the color of someone's skin.

If only people could open the doors
to where your departed soul rests!

To smell the burning embers
of churches destroyed
because others feared, out of ignorance,
the color of someone's skin.

If only people could open the doors
to where your departed soul rests!

And simply hear said with great honesty,
"Thank you, Martin Luther,
as God surely said, "My son! Job well done!"

If only people could open the doors
to where your departed soul rests!

And reclaim your vision,
your voice,
your mind,
your zest!
Renew the vision,
continue the talks,
invite the conversation.

If only people could open the doors
to where your departed soul rests!

Recall the plea for peace and equality,
for the work to continue toward a colorless society
here, there and everywhere on earth.

If only people could open the doors
… what a better world it would be!

Threads of life

Out of the primordial cosmos
we are steeped and grown in mother's womb
released into people's arms, held close,
with innocence, then instantly bloom.

Watching intently with our mind's-eye
we learned we are loved more, when we cry.
Toddling upward, we move closer to the sky.
As more years come, more years go by.

The college scene brought people to toast
as young lads and lassies bring on Love and doom
until we find the one who, we just know, we will love most.
We dated and lived large, perhaps, as a bride and groom.

We wrestled with careers, mortgages, and diapers not dry.
Watching, surviving, hearing the terrible twos' questions why,
as the teenagers' woes churn and make them and us cry.
Until they soon leave our nests and begin to solo fly.

So, retired now, with wise counsel,
we are careful not to quarrel,
as we watch our children's children being carefully groomed.

We do joyously acknowledge we have no regrets, no sorrows,
because in this Life, we have partaken waiting now for tomorrow.

Indistinguishability

Indistinguishable …
nature of being alike,
identical with self,
mirrored images
is selfsameness.
Reflection oneness
one
being identical with self.

Will my legacy be undone?

Pondering values I left for them,
obligations to not condemn.
Trusting the words that I wrote.
What's said can never be unspoke!

Over years, at my direction,
paths taken by my suggestions,
of sane reasoning for greed's poke.
What's said can never be unspoke!

Leaders plead at the journey's end,
please don't repeat what I would amend.
Those repeated words will not choke.
What's said can never be unspoke!

My desire is that it be known,
I used the intended words unminced
even when they made someone wince.
Yes the words were honestly spoken.
What's said can never be unspoke!

Reflecting, hiding any superstition,
reclaiming hope with strong conviction!
I led them far as their head spokesman.
What's said can never be unspoke!

Hopeless, my destiny

It's just not a typical city night
where all around seems to be alright.
The street is dark, the breeze is chilling.
I feel the stress of another killing.
See them preying in the lonely streets,
aware of too many people
who have succumbed to defeat.

Try as we do the death toll still rises
as a new drug king to the top arises.
We struggle for justice as a guiding light
but lose the innocent in the poverty fight.
Hope abandoned in the whine of voices

Forgo your hand-outs,
provide more choices!

Vessel of your prayer

Visions of Christ's hands
Eager to support
Sinners on their knees
Searching for God's Grace
Even through their wet tears
Lamenting for words.

Only heard in the heart
Forever clinging!

Youthful innocence
Opened to our first breaths
Understanding the Angels,
Reassurance of Grace!

Providing for all
Realizing the call.
Adhering solidly
Yielding to God
Every time, each day
Right with the "I AM."

Soul Friend

Friend,
Soul friend!
Listen, please
hear my sorrow.
My Anam Cara
help me move forward and
let words that part my lips soothe
tomorrow pains, my cheeks tear-stained
of despair, born in my soul does hurt.

Anam Cara, Soul Friend you never fail!
Good or sad times,
you have always been there.
Your companionship is like a salve
on an open wound that soothes the
fear, providing a healing,
compassionate safe space
where together we,
seeking God's Grace,
find
solace,
calm,
peace,
rest!

The park bench

Hush, can you hear the meadowlark's call?

The wind caresses spring's grasses, growing tall
as leaves budding forth promise a warm year.
The meadowlark's call, hush, can you hear?

People are strolling, eager to meet and greet,
as parents are helping little people cross the street.
On the grass, you see the dogs romping and rolling.
Eager to meet and greet, people are strolling.

On the park bench, I sit with my soulmate
chatting away about our lives being so great.
Then comes a rain shower, we get a drenching.
I sit with my sweet love on the park bench.

Hush, can you listen, as I whisper in your ear?
My lips softly read works of Shakespeare,
words fall into your heart from his pen.
I whisper in your ear, hush, can you listen?

The meadowlark soars up high in the sky,
then swoops down and looks us in the eye,
such calm, a safe space, sensing a rapport.
Up in the sky, the meadowlark soars …

Capture that silver lining

Capture that silver lining carefully.
Put in a safe place contained in a satin binding.
Tightly bound for the good of the human race.

Attend to our reckless habits!
Avoid falling into unhealthy ways.
Assist one and all on this planet.
Allow us to live our prescribed days.

Tell it from the mountain tops of
the tumultuous days, a world in peril,
trembling fear, worse than the pox!
Tragic deaths, from a bug gone viral.

Every day, we seek God's Divine plan.
Enemy and friend, together, fight this foe.
Tell this to all, so that we might forever
stand together, evermore united,
under God we will more spiritually grow.

Your halo

Such a privilege it is to see
the embodiment of Christ
that surrounds you like a halo.

Your selfless giving of time
and talents while being at
such uncertain risk shines in you.

Doctors, nurses, first-responders,
nursing home care providers,
the Godhead shines softly through.

During these tumultuous times,
it is all mankind that needs to
stand and shower the Light of kindness.

We are in this together
and together we will either
sparkle or fizzle.
Will we do our part for all of mankind?

Look in the mirror!
Seek in your heart
that warm glow,
the presence of God
under your softly shimmering halo.

Walking in solitude

Blustery, billowing winds bend leaves
and shake the very roots of trees.

'Tis so in the wisp of a gentle breeze
 when the blossoms bloom, I sneeze.

Little fawns nimble, nibble on grass
while the fox and the hare romp pass.

Bold stream gushes, rushes over boulders
while waterfall's mist tickles my shoulders.

Sunlight dances making a radiant rainbow
dancing, dazzling, putting on quite a show.

The shady mountain path wide, then narrow,
across the blue sky flies a host of sparrows.

A majestic eagle perches on a rocky crest
as eaglets neatly nestled in the nest rest.

I love Mother Nature's nurturing glory.
In my sacred solitude I write this story.

Boyish Love

Below the crest of yonder waterfall,
I sat and told you of this true love story.
As many years we were able to forestall,
this tale before my hair grew long and hoary.

And buried deep inside a slew of thoughts,
this maiden's cherry lips, boys have desired.
I sought her much more than I truly ought,
and I was burnt by kisses, as sparks fired.

Alas, life is chock full of silly laddies,
who learn to seek a lady they can love,
and boys look past the girls and bow to ladies.
A woman who is wise in life's ways fits hand to glove,

And yes, you wingless creature, near perfection,
you mirror all my love and true affection.

The hobo

This is the day I go away.
My only bag is by my side.
A pair of shoes had made me sway
but toes inside my shoes had died.
Holes in the soles repaired with glue.
A hand-me-down shirt, I just loved!
Jeans so worn the patches are torn.
Do not think I am feeling unloved.
The clothes on my back are not rags!

One thing for sure, I am quite glad
one change of wears has a new tag.
I think it best, be glad … than mad!

Up there … a spot I sought for years,
by a stream with lots of days that shine.
The oak full of leaves every year,
a roll of twine and bent wire, my fish line.
I have all that is needed to make a hook
for the daily fresh catch, that I will cook.

The whisper of words

Caught in the ink-black undertow of living
just one wrong step away
from a deepening abyss,
gripping tight-fisted
to the handrail of Life,
I struggle to stand firm on
this roiling, undulating patch of earth.

Not remembering how to take
a calming breath in a gentle breeze,
or simply go anywhere,
that would give me peace and comfort —
just to find stable ground,
which seems utterly hopeless —
then, only in that last instant …

looking heavenward,
into the blue-black depths of infinity,
beyond the wispy fog of a cluttered mind,
doing all I can to muster up the courage
buried deep within my savaged human vessel,
I wrestle with this thought …

Who or what, in that unknowable cosmos,
could be even capable or risk being culpable,
even daring, or caring enough
to make my patch in this world less shaky.

Suddenly, my eardrums vibrate from the
tolling of a hundred bells,
as my body and mind
continue reeling,
shaking my broken soul.

When, before my bleary tear-sodden eyes,
catching a slowly glowing whiteness that is
near blinding in its intensity, there, within,
is a God figure —

While the bells, now sit silent,
I hear the whisper of words —

Just Believe …

Just Believe …

Just Believe!

Reflections

Nowhere land

My thoughts spin as though
the reel of a well-cast fly line
sailing effortlessly outward …

I sit in the shadows of the underpass
in heavily tattered clothing and
jungle boots whose laces have long been frayed.

When was it?
Where I waded into that rushing stream,
just above the subtle backwater,
as the fly danced in the air toward the intended target.
The cool of the night creeps into the marrow of these now old bones
as I watch my breath swirl as a mist into the ever-darkening evening.

It was before boot camp,
and long before humping the boonies,
a site so deep in the jungle, we called it Nowhere land.

That rainbow trout practically jumped out of the river,
with trails of water gleaming in the sparkling golden rays of sun,
swallowing that hand-tied Caddisfly in one deep gulp.

I fold the mud smeared cardboard in half and
mold it under my arms for an extra layer of warmth
as I unscrew the cap on the half empty bottle of port.

Suddenly, I am in contest with this powerful fish,
I reel in as he gathers his strength and then he takes off,
the line zipping off the reel again, over and over, then snap.

I pull a long slow plug that burns my throat
clear down into the pit of a growling stomach
aching for a bit of hot chow.

Then, oh yes, then, I remember …
It was when the trout won,
I lost and here I am,
in Nowhere land.

Our human condition—suffering

Oh, how humanity's hearts, minds, bodies
exude the nasty moral turpitude of shameful acts …
stained on all of humankind.
Like dark inkblots throughout all recorded history.

Hatred, willful intolerance, destruction of
anything that does not conform to an
acceptable way of believing!

These acts are not new!
They chew away at the fiber of society
over time, like a moth that eats away fine silk.

These pitfalls for mankind have come and gone.
Throughout all of history,
in the near and far reaches
of every known place on earth,
as far back as the garden of Eden,
sucking the life out of lives.
Like quicksand unseen in the night,
pitfalls dot the human seascape.

Violent crimes against men, women and children
by those who are intolerant of anything
that portends to be for the good of all
is not new,
read any book of any religion.

The wisdom teachers, desert fathers and mothers
told story upon story of man's doing ill toward
their next-door neighbor.
Hearing the cock crow at the rising of another day of
man's heathen cries, *"I want it my way."*

Hailstorms of gunfire week in and week out,
pummel inner cities.
If not gunfire, choose a weapon of destruction
from any generation, back to and Cain and Abel,
you will see mankind's disgrace.
The selfish wanton acts have shredded
the very hearts of families, for eons of time,
shredded like the torn garments of a man
lost in a spiral down decline.

Black lives, brown lives, yellow lives,
white lives, red lives …
pick any one or all among these or more,
all people experience hurts, pains, sorrows,
regrets, ill will, disrespect, crashed dreams,
dashed hopes!

It is the human condition into which we are all born.

Such is the vast wasteland, dried and withering.
As time marches on to the tunes
of downtrodden drummers, we walk on.

Today, we have twenty-four seven news,
showing our failed human natures.

But our minds are now numbed
to see the bad, the ugly!
Some are thirsting even
to see one more horrible act not seen before.
Gut-wrenching, sour bile rising from the
depths of despair, all of us wanting change.

However, just as in the days of old
destruction of dreams is likened to the
turbulence of tornadic winds ripping homes
right off solid foundations.

This easily explains the jaw-dropping,
heart-wrenching, utter breath-restricting sights
unfolding before our very own eyes.

It has been the same for all of time recorded!

There are, have been and always will be people
who will rise and become leaders,
who have rent the very fabric of dignity
from fertile and healthy minds as they held
another fellow human down, because of greed.

Such are the persons who
thirst to hold those they attract
with their boisterous rhetoric,
while their purses are lined with gold.

They entice victims caught
in the swirling cesspool of failed
engineered systems that destroy
the very souls of people!

From man's beginnings to the
final fall of humanity,
these all carry the same human stain
brought about by their thirst for
money, power, and control.

For those who believe in a Divine order,
who live in the Present Moment, have a prayer life,
try to live within the containment
of the ten commandments —
they, I believe, have the greatest chance
to cling to the one element we must all hold
dear to our hearts.

Hope! That precious pearl, which stays hidden
in the soft belly of an oyster growing into
a softly gleaming gem, enables them to survive.

Hope.

Not penny loafers

Not penny loafers with scuffed heels,
nor my favorite to dance reels.
Too fast a pace dancing a jig,
they sure were not for chasing pigs.
Few words explain just how I feel!

The pennies stay put when I kneel
and make for comfortable wheels.
I prance around dry leaves and twigs
not in penny loafers!

While hearing the flying pig squeal,
copper, shining bright … so real
supple to touch, not worn by prigs,
certainly not any bigwigs
who would much prefer silver wigs
not penny loafers!

Celestial guardians

Oh, how longstanding my
guardians have stood
girded with their magenta sash
flung forth into the night skies,
creating dazzling sparkles lighting my path
within the depth of slumber and vivid dreams.

Stone-rigid protectors,
two on my right, gazing ever
upward and downward,
firm scowls and tight knit brows
emoting to the celestial travelers
make space for our nighttime sojourn.

Two guardians on my left
scanning forward and backward
emitting incredibly hard stares
toward any evil rogues roaming
from the depths of oncoming black holes
or past dark bottomless
crevices of Life's daytime burdens.

Center stage, there stood I.
Knowing from all directions
toward any path I so choose to try,
journeying as a celestial warrior,
seeking the wisdom path,
my every turn would be paved
with sure-footed sparkling stardust paths.
Thus, I smile so assuredly,
I travel safe,
my companions and I.

Run ... walk

Run,
run hard,
don't look back
for certain you'll
wobble, stumble, tumble,
go down …
so fast.

It's likely you'd scrape your big fat bottom.
What a sad sight
it would be
to see
you!

Walk,
walk slow,
a snail's pace
would be the trick!
simply slithering, dithering along.

Oh sure, it will take you so very long,
but rest assured,
take the time …
all you
need!

Tasks yet to do

God's tasks were assigned to me.
His breath of Life was my start
God's tasks were assigned to me.

A mystery, my task you see,
It took me years to listen in.
His breath of Life was my start.

So, trials and errors I partook,
but now I must do my part!
It took me years to listen in.

I did once have a running start
bent but surely not worn out,
now it's time, I must do my part!

More good days, sure to come
living large with borrowed days,
bent but surely not worn out!

Wondering, have I missed one?
God's tasks were assigned to me.

Living large with borrowed days,
God's tasks were assigned to me!

Tattered but not done

America,
are her
glory days gone?

Is it time to write a new song
for the home of a handful of people
whose causes trample on the legacy of generations
of the brave who fought and died,
just so and handful could have this day to say,
"I hate America, I hate you, I hate."

"We don't want the freedom you died for.
We want to tear down everything including history!"

No one can learn what price freedom costs,
unless they are prepared to sacrifice all.

To live without
laws and cops; no honor,
to let freedom be, no more, no more!"
"Burn it down, we say."

We know you are angry, so are we!
America stand!

A breath of fresh air

I so long for a breath of fresh air.
Do you?
Desire can be such a fleeting feeling.

However muddled, befuddled,
our thoughts become,
as we are consumed
by the constant onslaught of life's dramas
filled with people screaming
"You should have, you ought!"
Projecting scenes upon life's big screen,
that often takes our breath away.

I so desire to experience.
something so very unique,
so special, positively refreshing
that it does take your breath away
Do you?

Perhaps, you and I can begin
by sending a smile to a friend,
your neighbor, a colleague or
take a risk and let's high-five
a total stranger.

Now wouldn't that provide
a "breath of fresh air?"

Come on, will you take the dare?

Beyond the blue sky

'Tis no wonder that, faithfully, I cast my gaze
heavenward into the deep blue yonder.
To sneak a peek into the unknown, not seen,
masked by the bluest of skies,
searching for a moment of tranquility and calmness

that slows the rhythm of my heart thumping.

At night, my mind's eye,
sailing through blue oceans of dreams
on waves, at times, light blue —
my guardians and I set sail,
seeking healing and understanding.

Traveling further into darkest blue
of nighttime cosmic travel,
clinging to a seriousness,
seeking knowledge,
how to point my life toward that one,
bright, guiding star
that twinkles like a dazzling sapphire
cut so perfectly.
The image behaves as beveled glass,
projecting into infinity,
guiding my soul onward.

How I write free verse

If you were my morning guest
you might see excitement dawning,
or if you could magically slide inside my head
absorbing juicy tidbits, as if a dry sponge in the desert sun,
seeing first-hand how my free verse is done.

My day, surrounded by stillness, begins.
Sometimes starting out gray, then turning brighter,
as if I can dial up just the right amount of daylight for warmth.

Mind swirling within a current thought,
or tiptoeing around a harsh memory, at times,
I lightly caress a deep feeling that trickles
like a small stream beginning a downward flow.

Keyboard set, coffee cup brimming,
my well-worn Webster's near,
I let words begin spiraling upward from deep within
my soul onto the page.

Word images, blood red when read,
harsh memories can bring a tear,
words creating an ebb and flow,
a tension, pulling the string taut on a longbow,
while adding a touch of yin and yang,
send a pause for the reader to
consider … this or that.

Like adding a bit of zest when preparing a feast,
I drop in a poetic device or two,
interwoven like delicate lace.
Then I add a touch of gold or silver
for a well-constructed piece.

Tossing in assonance creating the effect … despair,
as in the ripping open my heart for love gone asunder.
something we might share in common?

If welcomed into the verse,
I might sprinkle in a dash of onomatopoeia.
As in a cuckoo when the sweet bird's refrain
is heard at the top of the hour.

Then pausing for a day or two,
I leave the words to stew
wanting the verse to subtly entice you.

When I read and reread the written tome,
perhaps massage a stiff word in a stanza or more,
it is then I must make a decision …
is this good enough to serve to you?

Infinite

Just imagine …
mentally drawing a ring,
no matter how big or small,
worry not, even if it is as big
as a hula hoop.

Now, picture in your mind's eye
you are beginning a journey …
just as you take a step into this circlet —
shimmering iridescently, appearing
as a golden halo past the exosphere —
you enter into deep space.

Then, just lightly exhale as you take
the next step inside this circle.
Your breath is like a tiny jet stream
of energy that creates the motion of a
spiral rotating away from the entrance of
an annulus into the cosmic stew
toward this galaxy and beyond.

Boundless into infinity,
your circle revolves around an
encompassed sea of stars which
circle ever more infinitely
into space, as you trustingly take that
next step.

You just had a life cycle experience
within a circle!

Eye for an eye

Heartbreak's refrain
eye for an eye, why?
On a river of wounds,
tears flow on endlessly.

Bow ties, silk ties, family ties

How my world has changed!
Such a seeker I once was for that perfect
colorful silk fashion statement just for an upcoming event.

With much forethought and mental dancing, I stood wondering
just how much preening and prancing was needed to create the outfit.

Willing always to appreciate the personal statement worn by others,
but, of course, hoping theirs did not out-do mine!

Any professional, will relate to that perfect power tie
especially selected, such a projection of boldness,
like wearing a swordsman's chainmail into the boardroom
battle to prevent one being eviscerated in a struggle!

Then for the lighthearted occasion,
the gentlemen favoring a more genteel time.
An event, perhaps, more formal,
one would presume a bowtie would be most common.

Unless, of course, you were a Texan, fixin' to go two-steppin'.
Then that bolo, with a shining silver slide
and turquoise stone, would be beholden of a second look.

Alas, all good things do pass!
No one really can place a practical purpose for a tie,
just like jewelry, or cosmetics, or a well-placed tattoo,
piercings in body parts seen … well, unseen too,
high heels or that gentleman's pocket square.

Truly, it is kind of like waving a flag,
the ego does thrive, when showing respect,
or running with the herd
creating a sense of belonging,

then again,
one could be thinking of
possibly more dangerous kind of ties ... .

family ties,
which would require a
whole new outfit and beginning.

Passing through your Life

My soul is bruised, my heart is bleeding
the last spoken words that I was pleading
making a crevasse with no crossing back,
plummeting into the deepening black,
to your selfish wants I wasn't conceding.

Those spoken words felt so misleading
had you just tried …
I'd have given some slack.
My soul is bruised.

I felt your soft touch, your warmth receding
creating doubts, I knew you were succeeding.
I tired so, of the constant unfettered flack
my love song's refrain was not misleading.
My soul is bruised.

Just passing through, no destination known.
Thinking our love bond was tightly sown
but I knew your Love was held restrained
as freedom I needed to once again attain.
Just passing through.

No, I walk through this gate alone.
Underfoot I walk on sharp stones.
In relationships — closeness strained.
Just passing through.

Silly how little I want to bemoan
or feel the need to cry out a groan.
Lamenting, I need to learn to abstain
from companionship when I create pain.
Accepting that it is my Life I must own.
Just passing through.

Reflecting

I still stand often in
this mountain stream
catching my reflection,
while reflecting upon
bygone days.

Ghost writer

I heard the whoosh …
I saw the wick on the taper flicker
I felt a chill in the air,
just as the quill began dancing across
the slightly yellowed linen paper milled using water and rags.

Suddenly, a ghostly figure evolved
hunched over my deeply scarred writing table
with the bib of the quill dipped in the jet black ink well.

With a flourish of motion,
the quill seemed to float buoyantly
along the less than smooth surface of paper
scratching a cursive line of a script that
read, "write — write — write,"

The ghost of times past appeared to look
over its lowered shoulder, toward me,
gazing ever so intently, and continued to scrawl
as these words appeared, "words tell the story,
my story … must be told, be bold, take up my quill,
before you grow too old.

You must tell my story!"

Star falling

Star
falling,
certain death
lighting the sky.
I ponder, why must
such a lonely passing
be witnessed by such as I?
My thoughts are not known,
wondering whose soul passes
by from east to west!
Is this departure seen
by more than me?

On the spectrum

From the very beginning,
the sense that this little lamb
was seeing his new world
from a different lens was real!

The distraction of a mobile,
twirling above his head,
sending this little lion into terrible fits
of what seemed pain-driven terror.

A splashing of water on this precious
little gift of Life anywhere near his face,
would cause sensations of what appeared
to make him act like it was scalding water —
although cool as a soothing drink.

For fourteen years I have seen with
my own eyes, the signs of his "peaking,"
his collision with just too much activity,
causing him to melt down into a primordial
stew of fear and uncontrollable tension.

But the tears come to my eyes
when I watch this young Einstein
take on the monumental task of building
the most demanding Lego projects
one can imagine possible with little locking
blocks. No instructions wanted/needed.

Not once, but over and over and yet over again
with a smile as wide as a battleship turning
into the wind, he builds and builds the same things
again and again.

I know then in my heart,
that God has kissed this child becoming a man,
and know that he is just fine —
my grandson, just being John.

Light from many sources

As I bade goodbye to the sparkling dance of Light
from a million stars across my pre-dawn sky,
my anticipation amped up as I caught
the very first projections
of golden illumination gathering speed,
rising with brilliant radiance,
hiding that backdrop of starlight
while the new day's rays of daylight
covered over the last phosphorescence
of the moonlight glow.

It is then that I just knew
that the nearby streetlight would suddenly extinguish
its warm projection of light seen within the fading shadows.

A stroll in the woods

Stroll in the woods
woods moist with dew
dew glistening in the Light
Light that turns our heads to,

    to quickly cover our faces, zip and snap
    snap snug about our chins
    chins tucked under the collars
    collars so high it covers our grins,

        grins, as we go through the forest
        forest deep, dark, and cold
        cold as the breeze blows strong
        strong and steady we are fearlessly bold,

            bold and brave we continue our pace,
            pace we set to stay abreast of the Light.
            Light that ebbs and flows from the leaves' steady dance,
            dance, as we twirl like dervishes whose hearts are bright.

Another decade

Turn the page,
a decade is gone!
Start anew!

Near summer's end

Summer days ebb and flow
each day shortening the depth of Light
expanding into the evening night
as the sun sets in the western sky.

At the end of a summer's day
as the waves slowly slink away
I saunter with the warm water licking my thighs
digging into my thoughts of, Why?

Pushing along with gliding steps
letting my soul reach into deeper depths
pondering the lingering days of summer's sunny rays.
Questioning what is to come in the following days?

Transitions

Fall's colors are in full swing
as leaves change the summer scene.

In a matter of a few short weeks
it has gone from very green peaks
to shrouded trees and very gray skies
while many colorful birds chirp goodbyes.

As morning creeps into the dark night's view
a dose of chilled air brings shivers to you.

'Ere, stoking the hearth by stirring the embers
stirs you to split more wood before December.

The garden has produced its final crop
'tis time to let it rest as growth did stop.

I sip a cup of coffee marveling at such as this
certain other seasons do not provide as much bliss.

November's beaver moon

November's Beaver moon hung low in the night sky.
The harsh cold air held tight to the heavy
mist following the mountain stream
into the still shadows of the forest beyond.
Many times, I have lingered by these
outcroppings of rock clinging to
the bank of this stream.
My heartbeat slows to match
the rhythm of the pace of nature
while at restful sleep.

Thoughts stir, unwinding, like silent reels whirling
of bygone days when you sat beside me.

These unwelcomed thoughts, opening up deep-set pangs of loneliness.
You may know that same feeling of loneliness one senses
when hearing the evening call of the lone whippoorwill
pleading for a mate to reply.

That solo call matches this moon phase's tenor
separating the winter solstice,
reminding me of the cycles of Life we once shared.

Remembering the warmth of your breath as it tickled my ear lobe
while you whispered sweet words of Love.
This was then a space in time when we were so much alive
and quite literally unbeatable in any of life's many games.

As I watched the clouds of mist reveal more of the low-hung moon,
pondering more deeply about the coming of the next full moon
and all the mysteries of life, that moon too
will shine forth unto this mortal soul.

Wonder fills me with the question,
just how many ways can the moon present
a sneak-peek without a passport to travel?

He and She

He and She visit me everyday.
I never cease to be in awe
of their display of companionship.

He will sing a sweet tune and
while away time,
until she arrives
and shares his limb.

His feathers red,
hers speckled white and black,
far from blended in
the forest green
pretending not to be seen.

As October nights chill
the air, on the tips of leaves,
abiding the cold,
put on a color show
ever so bold.

The cardinals, both he and she
are blending more fully
in the rusting of leaves,
I watch until,
at last,
they too leave.

Time out

Sometimes, I simply feel the need
to unplug, deprogram, unstress,
just take a time out.

Life tosses more at us than we can …
as they say, "Say Grace over,"
but really there is so much more
in store and mostly it is all a bore.

We can jump and shout
and I might even want to pout
and, oh! the amount we heap deep
onto our plates in twenty-four hours
makes things creepy.

It used to be meetings, and airports,
a conference or two
more than I wanted to do.
But now, it's Zoom in a room
and hoping the lighting
doesn't make me look pale
or stale or worst-case frail.

Winter Shadows (Kyrielle)

Hours of winter darkness creep slow
causing some to draw deep within!
The lack of light and they lay low.
Winter shadows linger longer.

Nature's twist of lighter later
some people sit with head-on-chin.
Wintry days serve the sun hater.
Winter shadows linger longer.

The solo yard light is still aglow.
Hoarfrost on the windowpanes
spins tendrils of a dancing rainbow.
Winter shadows linger longer.

This season begins to soon pass.
Sun rises earlier again,
pushing darkness away at last.
Winter shadows linger longer.

Memories

Dream or ghostly visit?

As I sit beside the driftwood fire,
wind tousling my wavy thin gray hair,
my thoughts flow, matching rhythm
with gentle waves licking the soft sand, retreating,
repeating again and ever more nature's dance.

All the while, moonbeam light pairs with the fire,
a prism catching the Light from above and below,
showering the distant stretch of shore in soft Light,
white on white but, subtle to enhance memories
repeating eves spent 'oft at this time, in this space,
flowering once again, those blissful embraces
of times when spent by your side
feeling full of Love's sweet nectar
teasingly wet my lips,
as we gaze at the night.

When suddenly, a whisper that teases me
to then focus on the shift of wind stamping out moonbeam rays
as large clouds shroud the moon
and large waves cascade in, the fire's glow tamps down.
Strangely the specter looms above the flickering flame
of the red-hot blaze, and the whole scene startles me,
awakening me, toppling me back to the fire, wind, waves.
This happenstance, this sudden, ghostly guest
puts goose bumps on my skin.

Graveyard by the sea

The October mist swirls in from the seashore
bringing a wet chill that sets deep in the night watchman's
bones on this All Hallows' Eve.

His torch flickers, in the whisper of wind,
dancing, bobbing, and weaving gently,
as tendrils of soft Light bleed into the heavy dark shadows.

A blood-curdling scream unsettles the rhythm
of the croaking frogs calling out to their prospective mates.
The flurry of sound from flapping wings as the startled
flock of marsh hens rushed into the depth of night.
adds to the sudden quake felt in the time-worn
hands of this trusted sentinel of the graveyard by the seashore.

Suddenly, the mist turns into a heavy fog that carries in its white
shroud, enveloping every crypt, the dank smell of seaweed.

Then the undeniable sound, ding-ding, ding-ding,
signaling two bells, like from a tall ship at sea, that long ago,
would had been tied to the wharf in the bay.

As the watchman pulled out his timepiece
seeing with amazement that it was, indeed, two in the morn.
At that very instant there came a long deep and pain-filled moan from
just past the outreaches of his sight.

She appeared,
as if floating just above the pebble laden pathway
with her arms outstretched fingers on both hands
signaling an invitation to come — come here.

Shaking his head no,
this seasoned veteran of two score and five all Hallows' eves,
simply nods and says, "I bid farewell, you damsel from the sea,
I know you are a lost soul, so just pass well into the dark,
rest well, 'til next All Halloween."

Lover's Quarrel

Dare he reclaim her calm,
therein dispel chagrin?
Or doth she break,
her heart soon ache?

Wouldst they reflect upon
unsaid thoughts each misread,
while stings persist amid clenched fists?

A deep morass awaits this pair
unless they dare embrace,
renew their resolve,
thus, fear subdue.

Yuletide

Yuletide …
peppermint drops,
treetops twinkling,
sugar plums sparkling,
Christmas songs sung loud,
children laughing,
their grandparents tearing,
mom busy spiking dad's eggnog,
warm fire glows in near hearth.
I send greetings
Yuletide!

Bedecked, but for naught

Our home all bedecked
the Douglas fir scent fills the air,
stockings hung with great care.
The children's favorite carols checked.
Silent Night ready for all to share.
Gifts made ready, bows and ribbons here and there.
We sit at the ready, the lists all rechecked
rocking together, we reminisce of memories that flare,
when into the warm hearth we both suddenly stare.
With the feeling of anguish,
we both feel sadness crashing in waves
as we drop a tear,
our grandchildren, due to Covid,
can't come this year.

Christmas morn

Christmas stockings all hung with great care
the gifts, under the tree, even a new teddy bear.

Milk half gone, just cookie crumbs on the plate
remnants of treats, left for Santa, as they went to bed late.

The sparking lights and tinsel so shimmery
lighting the way for St. Nick's slide down the chimney.

But the best to be seen were those eye-popping stares
as each of the grandchildren came down the stairs.

The warmest delight that a grandpapa might savor
is gathering all around and reading without a quaver
the story about the birth of our Savior.

Dedicating another Christmas for the best gift that could
be teaching our children His gift is better than any under the tree!

Frolicking

Oh, what a blast!
Rubbing the stardust from my just-opened eyes,
I gazed widely, with a sense of sudden joy,
out the nearby window seeing before me
more snow than I have ever seen ever.

Dashing like Donner and Blitzen
to the closet to find just the right clothes,
I put on those without one pause,
followed just as smartly donning
those woolly woolens to keep my toes warm.

Then, hopping like a bunny in a garden patch,
I rushed out the door to begin a day of fun galore!
A plop in the snow to make
it known to all that on this grand day,
I had come to fully enjoy the thrills,
and spills hoping I had my Angel wings sewn on!

The red sled, which sped faster than the blue toboggan,
made the trips down the slope quite a thrill.

Trip after trip so slick all I could do
was trill out a lout shrill shriek!

Oh, what fun, snow and hill and friends do make!

Arctic blast

Squeak, squeak, squeak,
the snow so cold each step resounds!
The mist from someone's breath
becomes tiny icy crystals at once,
falling with almost a hint of a
tinkle, tinkle as they hit the ground.

That hoarfrost still creeping
even as the noon-day sun
begins its brief afternoon run.

While the calendar is stuck in the muck
as wet fingers are glued to Tuesday,
and you can't turn the page.

Imagine it so cold
that the just-poured hot chocolate
is already slushy!

One can only hope that the earth
will continue its revolutions on pace
to get us past this wintery scene.

Perchance, do you have an extra blanket?
If not, some heavy long johns
will certainly do.

And if not asking too much …
a nice steamy bowl of very spicy chili
and some corn bread too!

Twenty below with snow

When it is twenty below with snow
or warning of a blow
surely have ready a ton of coal
and grandma's hand-made throw,
socks on toes.

Don't forget to stack wood by the hearth,
wise to wear a warm scarf,
put extra bedding on the low berth
stay dry for all you're worth,
socks on toes.

Stoking hearth aglow with a wood fire
keeping matches drier in the pockets of winter attire
wear gloves that you desire,
socks on toes.

Should the roads close 'tis best stay in the house
and snuggle tighter with spouse.
Hug her tighter when she spots a mouse.
Hunker down, cook a grouse,
socks on toes.

The blizzard of sixty-eight

In sixty-eight the lightning took out the mighty oak!
The shock was not the loss of the tree,
the shock came because it was on December twelve
when it snowed and snowed and snowed.

Four nights came and five days went
as snow measured from waist-deep to eaves tall
tunnels were dug to get out the big and small.
In sixty-eight the lightning took out the mighty oak!

Not a car was to be seen, nor a snowplow could go.
People were in awe of the very deep snow.

The shock was not the loss of the tree!

Most natives warned it was bad as could be,
the snow just piled and piled, burying all the trees.
Then concerns rose about no Christmas possibly.
The shock came because it was December twelve.

So much snow, nowhere to go,
there wasn't space to begin to plow.
When we thought the worst was finally over,
then it snowed and snowed and snowed.

What Love is

Love, the foundation
the brick and mortar that
the building blocks of
one's highest and best
Self has to give.

Who gains from Love
given without any shackles?
No interest demands,
No late payments.
Not even an expectation
to receive Love given?

All, each and everyone
gains a little more humanness
from the gift of compassion,
the act of forgiveness,
the offering of patience,
the maturation of tolerance,
the showering another with affection.

These and much more are
rewards for one who is anchored
in the heart, mind and soul
while in the harness of Love.

Love is all of this and more.

Retrospections

The Master's messenger

In the silence, I sit …
My heart's desire is to shut out
the several fluttering thoughts. Save but just one.

"Why have you, Master, allowed this human being to survive this long?"
My thought …
I have heard the sweet music float as though on a cloud,
from a harp with gold-laden strings.

Where the Light emitted through my tears being shed
for all those years of shying away from your voice,
your constant invitation to just seek,
is near blinding in its dazzling, pure brilliance.

My thought continues …
Father, Mother, God. This humble child of the great I AM
has stilled my soul to receive
that which You have to give unto me …
When suddenly a dove,
as white as the purest flakes of snow,
lands ever so slowly upon the near window sill,
and it is at that moment,
I just know …
that the one called by ninety-nine names
has sent this messenger to show me I have Angels in my presence.
Master has sent His Goodness. There I find Peace!

> *My thought …*
> *A harp with gold-laden strings, In pure harmonic brilliance,*
> *you have to give unto me. Then I just know!*

I have Angels in my presence.
Master has sent His Goodness.
There I find Peace!

Forgive oneself

Mistakes entrap the mind!
Also, regrets attached to past deeds.
There sit I, stalled deep in Life's weeds
where hurt and remorse do breed.
Malaise keeps me in a taut bind.

My once champagne and roses, big plans, derailed.
Irate at self for all the attempts that failed,
the weight of injustice wrongly scaled.

So whence did that week, day, hour grind
my dreams, my hopes, to halt, thus I declined?
Oh yes! There were many days and all manner
of ways where I stepped so high my soul
soared fine, and I had far more ups than downs,
then it all near magically turned sour.

Mistakes entrap the mind unless one can forgive oneself,
be it himself or it could be herself!
Life sure does not flow like a flat ocean
So do prepare, hold on, be ready for all the commotion.

Mistakes do not need to entrap the mind
nor does malaise keep me in a taut bind!

Resting place

Tragedy often strikes unforeseen.
As one stands on hallowed ground
often, all that comes to mind are the whys,
with no whisper of answers heard in the
softest of breezes wheezing as warm air teases
the flower petals woven into the near wreath.

These hallowed grounds were visited
when I had losses ten years before
and will likely be seen again ten years after,
as families gather for final farewells uttered in silence
having been too far away to say last goodbyes.

So, it just is …
ten years have come and gone
the blades of grass far from appearing
uniformly trimmed.

The tree has grown thicker, taller. Its canopy
shading yonder resting souls, with shadows
dancing on the breeze that helps cool the air.

The changes aplenty, ten years passing, hence the
need for me to be guided to the proper place
to stand once again, my knees now creakier,
my hearing less tuned to the honking flock of geese
flying over toward a near pond.

My memory teases thoughts more slowly these days,
retelling scenes from the last time I stood on these
hallowed grounds.

Then, as now, I am still awaiting my time
to once again be beside you forevermore.

Sacred contracts

What does surrender look like?

Wisdom has poured through the hourglass of time
for eons upon eons, like the sand sifting across the desert.

Spiritual masters — Abraham, Jesus, Buddha, Muhammad,
and all those unseen, unheard Wisdom teachers
before these, and those who come after,
are the gatekeepers of your Higher Purpose.

The seeker must abandon the death grip on earthly treasures,
bound up in the egotistic striving to store up
and hoard material possessions,
those money-grubbing, bourgeois habits.

If you are the seeker and you desire to be
an unrestrained explorer,
freed from self-imposed shackles,
search for, and then shine Light onto
your Sacred Contract. Then surrender!

Yield from fear and worry,
do not succumb to wants and desires,
go deep into your Higher Self,
quiet your selfish thoughts, and be Still.

Allow the ripples in the waves of Life's streams
to make sounds like music from a harp
gently moving you toward the Light
that shines brilliantly on the purpose
and the meaning of your Life.

When you see the Light,
then your most significant challenge will be
to know that your Spiritual Contract
will bring about your most intriguing
challenges and opportunities
to live into your Spiritual commitments.

Then, drink deeply from the calm waters
of your Life stream
and live into your fullest and highest abilities.

This is what surrender looks like!

Made in the USA
Columbia, SC
14 March 2021